The Great Tree Mouse Adventure

Martin Waddell

Illustrated by Wilbert van der Steen

This is Little and Small and No-Size-At-All before their Great Tree Mouse Adventure.

The three mice lived under the roots of a tree in a large forest. They were safely hidden under their tree until, one day, the roots shook and . . .

Down came their tree and all the other trees in the forest.

Somehow . . .

. . . they escaped, but when they came out, their whole world had gone.

"We've got to leave here right now," Small told Little.

So the three mice set out on their journey to find a new home. Small and Little took turns to carry No-Size-At-All because No-Size-At-All was too tiny to walk very far.

There were broken roots and big boots and machines all around them.

“Where shall we go?” Little squeaked.

“We’ll go this way,” decided Small.

But they didn’t get very far before they came to …

a raging bush fire!

Somehow . . .

. . . they escaped through the flames and the smoke, though their tails and their whiskers were singed.

When the three mice had recovered, they started walking again.

"Which way shall we go?" Little squeaked.

"This way!" said Small, though she didn't really know where to go.

Someone had to decide, so Small did.

Soon they came to a creek, but the three little mice couldn't swim. Small thought they could hop across from one stone to another.

"We might fall in and drown!" cried Little.

"We'll just have to risk it," said Small.

Small and Little held on to No-Size-At-All, but then Small slipped and . . .

SPLASH!

Somehow . . .

. . . they reached the far bank. They lay for a while in the mud, tired and cold, but they knew they had to go on.

As night came, the mice walked on.

On and on they walked, and then, suddenly, they saw . . . a cat!

"Help!" squeaked Little.

"Run!" yelled Small.

Somehow . . .

. . . they escaped, though Little got scratched and Small almost lost the tip of her tail.

“Which way now?” Little asked Small.

“I don’t know,” said Small.

So Little climbed up a broken fence post, and then . . . the moon rose.

“I can see tree tops far away!” Little squeaked.
“Then that’s where we’re going,” said Small.

Little and Small took turns carrying No-Size-At-All. Sometimes the tiny mouse walked by himself, though his short legs couldn't go very fast.

On and on they walked, past an old shoe, across some stones, over a log, down one side of a ditch and up the other.

“I can’t walk much further,” Little squeaked.

“We **have** to go on,” Small told Little.

They went on and on, on and on, on and on.

And then . . .

"**TREES!**" gasped No-Size-At-All.

At last, the three mice had reached the end of their journey.

The mice searched among the tree roots for somewhere to make their new home.

"This one?" said Little.

"That one?" said Small.

But it was No-Size-At-All who found the best place, where the tree roots were just right for small mice to dig.

They made their new home by scratching and digging about.

It is a safe place for small mice to be, and they're living there still.

Somehow . . .

. . . they had found a new home.